Nut
Skin, H;

OTHER BOOKS IN THIS SERIES:

NUTRITION

FOR

Skin, Hair, and Nails

•

JUDITH SWARTH, MS, RD
AND THE HEALTH MEDIA
EDITORIAL PANEL

foulsham
LONDON • NEW YORK • TORONTO •
SYDNEY

foulsham

Yeovil Road, Slough, Berkshire SL1 4JH

ISBN 0–572–01722–7

Copyright © Slawson Communications Inc. 1992

This British Edition © W. Foulsham & Co Ltd

Printed in Great Britain by
St Edmundsbury Press Ltd, Bury St Edmunds, Suffolk.

Contents

Contents

Introduction

Skin, hair, and nails depend on a constant supply of nutrients from the blood to maintain function and health.

Poor nutrition means that the nutrients required are not available, and the results are lifeless, dull, brittle hair; dry, red or cracked skin; and nails that break easily. Beauty starts from within.

Beauty depends on both good physical and emotional health; nutrition is important in maintaining both.

This book will explain the causes of nutrition-related symptoms and explore other aspects of diet and environment that cause changes in the health of skin, hair, and nails.

1

Beauty from Within

The skin, hair, and nails are an outer reflection of internal health; their texture, moisture, smell, temperature, and colour are the reflections of a person's well-being.

Clear skin, shiny hair, and firm pink nails are signs of a healthy, well-nourished body. Skin, hair, and nails reflect many aspects of both health and disease. Nutritional deficiency symptoms that are evident in these tissues can alert an individual to problems.

What Is Skin?

The soft, thin covering of the human body is both vulnerable and strong. It forms a barrier to some substances in the environment, but is permeable to others.

The three layers, and between 12 and

20 square feet of surface, make skin the largest organ in the body. Skin contains more than a quarter of the body's protein and accounts for about 12% of the body's weight, which is about seven pounds in the average adult. Skin is tough, resilient, and has the ability to repair itself when damaged. Skin is an important defence against foreign substances and parasites, it is a channel for elimination of body waste products, and it prevents unnecessary loss of fluids from the body.

Numerous substances can cross from the environment into the body through skin. It is particularly permeable to fat-soluble substances. Some medications are administered through the skin because of the ability of the skin to absorb and slowly then release substances into the blood. Toxic compounds also can pass through the skin, which is why attention must be paid to warnings about the use of some chemicals.

The Layers Of The Skin

The skin consists of three layers: the subcutaneous, the corium (dermis), and the outer epidermis that is seen in the mirror. These layers also are called the "under-skin", and "skin", and "overskin." The thickness of the skin varies over the body and is thickest on the palms, bottoms of the feet, and elbows. The skin on the eyelids is thin to allow easy movement and flexibility.

The Subcutaneous: The deepest layer of the skin, the subcutaneous, is a resilient cushion of fat and collagen. Collagen is a component of the fibrous, connective tissue that holds cells together. This layer of fat cushions internal organs and bones from shock, temperature changes, and physical impact. The average person has approximately 35 pounds of subcutaneous fat. Blood vessels and lymph channels feed into the subcutaneous layers. Hair follicles and some nerve endings extend to this layer. *(Figure 1, page 12)*

Hair growth originates in the deep layers of the skin. The hair root extends into the subcutaneous layer where it is surrounded by a specialised structure called the hair follicle. The hair follicle is a thin pouch-like outgrowth of the outer layer of the skin, the epidermis. Connected to the hair follicle are glands called sebaceous glands that secrete oils and lubricate the hair,

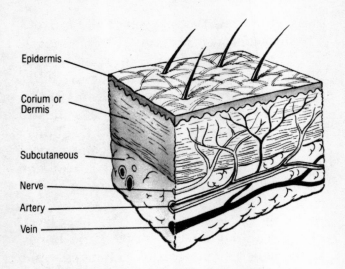

Epidermis

Corium or
Dermis

Subcutaneous

Nerve

Artery

Vein

Figure 1: The Layers of the Skin

The skin consists of three principal layers, the subcutaneous, the corium (dermis), and the outer epidermis.

nails, and skin. The combination of these oils with dead skin cells is called sebum. Sebum keeps hair glossy and the skin supple and might help defend the skin from bacterial infection. Other examples of sebum include earwax and dandruff. Sebum production is greater in men than in women because of the effects of the male hormone testosterone on the production of these oils. Abnormal production of sebum can contribute to acne. (See pages 64–67)

Subcutaneous tissue serves as a shock absorber, as a heat insulator, and as a reserve of calories in the form of fat. When body fat is measured, the instrument used, called skinfold calipers, pinches this layer of fat to assess the percent of overall body fat.

The Corium: The middle layer of the skin, called the corium or dermis, is considered the "true" skin. The corium shields underlying layers of the skin from injury and repairs surrounding layers when they are damaged. The upper portion of this layer has an abundant supply of blood and nerve endings. The top layer of the corium contains blood vessels that supply the hair follicles with oxygen, nutrients, and blood. These blood vessels also help regulate body temperature.

The corium stores water, minerals, and blood. Nerves that stimulate the muscles and cause goose bumps to form and hair to stand erect when the body is cold or frightened are located in the corium. These nerves also stimulate the release of fluids and oils from glands that are embedded in the corium.

Wrinkles originate in the corium. Collagen bundles and elastic fibres intertwine to form a pattern called Langer's lines that coincide with the normal creases of the skin.

The Epidermis: The outer or top layer of the skin is called the epidermis. The epidermis is the thinnest layer of the skin. It is about the thickness of a few pages of a book. The nails, hair, and toenails grow from the epidermis. *(Figure 2, opposite)*

As in all tissues of the body, the epidermis is composed of cells. The three main cells of the epidermis are keratinocytes, melanocytes, and Langerhans cells. Keratinocytes manufacture the protein keratin. Melanocytes produce the pigments that colour skin. Langerhans cells are components of the immune system and aid in the body's defence against infection and disease.

There are several layers within the epidermis. The bottom layer, closest to the corium, produces new cells that move upward as dead cells are lost each day. The entire process, from the production of new cells to those cells being sloughed

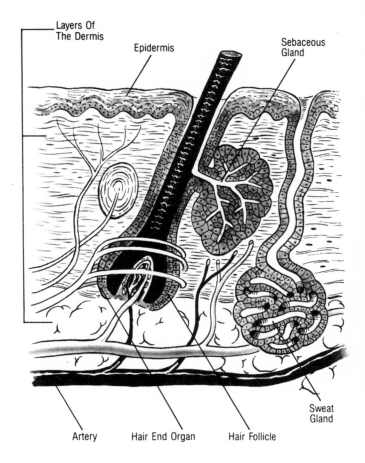

Figure 2: The Epidermis and Dermis Layers of the Skin

off, takes about one month. The innermost layer of the epidermis also contains the pigment cells (melanocytes) that give the skin its colour.

Keratin is responsible for the ability of the skin to provide a physical barrier against chemicals, parasites, and other foreign substances. In contrast, the Langerhans cells destroy harmful substances that invade the skin. Covering all the layers of the skin is a layer of dead keratinised cells. These cells swell in response to moisture and are shed daily.

What Are Nails?

Nails are composed primarily of a dense, dry protein and are approximately 5% fat. They have a very low water content, which accounts for their hardness. The body portion of the nail, which lies exposed on the ends of our fingers and toes, is extended at the base under the skin and rests on the nailbed. The pale, crescent-shaped area at the base of the nail is the lunala, named for its resemblance to the moon or luna. The activity of the cells at the nail base causes the nail to grow both in length and

thickness. Growth rate averages one milli-
meter per week, slows in the summer, and
increases in the winter. Rate of growth is
also affected by hormones, state of health,
nutrition, and age.

What Is Hair?

Hair is thin and flexible and different in
texture from skin even though both contain
the protein keratin. The hair shaft is
embedded in a cavity called the follicle.
This cavity is surrounded by tiny blood
vessels called capillaries that nourish the
hair and supply it with oxygen, vitamins,
minerals, water, and other nutrients.
Capillaries also remove waste products.
These capillaries are narrow branches of
the same blood vessels that bring blood
to neighbouring skin tissue. Oil-secreting
glands, called sebaceous glands, are also
attached to the follicle. These release a
constant supply of oils (sebum) to nourish
and moisten the hair shaft. *(Figure 3, page
18)*
  The hair shaft consists of more than one
layer of the cells. The outermost is termed
the cuticle, the middle layer the cortex,

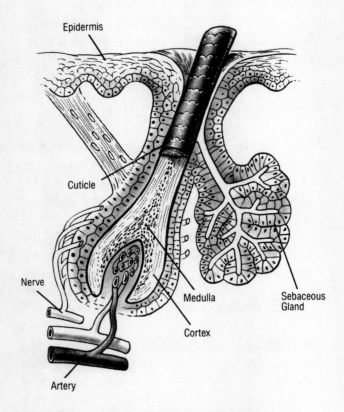

Figure 3:   The Hair Shaft and Follicle

and the central core the medulla. The middle layer is the main protein-rich portion of the hair, and hair colour is determined by the various blonde, brown, red, or black pigments it contains. If this middle layer does not contain pigment then white hair is the result. Hair is shed at different rates in different parts of the body; hair loss and growth is a constant process. Eyebrow hairs last only three to five months. Hair of the scalp lasts two to five years. Baldness results when growth of new hair is not adequate to replace hair that is lost.

2

Nutrients that Maintain Well-Nourished Skin, Hair, and Nails

Protein and Calories

Muscles are broken down for energy when consumption of protein or calories is not adequate to meet the body's needs. The muscles attached to the bottom surface of skin normally contribute to a firm skin tone. When the underlying muscles deteriorate from lack of protein and calories, the skin becomes slack. The fat stores of the skin also are depleted to provide energy. This leaves the skin thin and inelastic. The result is an emaciated or "skin and bones" appearance.

A diet severely deficient in protein also might result in a loss of proteins in the blood that attract and hold water. When these circulating proteins become low, water moves from the blood into the tissues, where it causes swelling known as oedema. This gives the skin a puffy, swollen look, and can hide the underlying deterioration of the muscle and fat tissues.

Deficiency of protein and calories causes changes in hormones and other regulators of body processes. Alterations in hormones can cause the skin to look shiny, thin, dry, and develop brownish spots. Hair loss is likely. Hair loses its lustre, becomes short and dry, and is easily and painlessly plucked from the scalp. Hair loss and muscle loss have been noted in dieters who do not consume sufficient protein or calories to meet their daily needs. Severe protein-calorie malnutrition in children causes hair to turn orange, which is caused by pigment changes in the hair shaft.

In order to maintain muscle tone, the diet must contain adequate protein and enough calories so that the body does not use either the dietary protein or the protein present in muscle tissue for energy. In addition, the muscles must be exercised. Without exercise the muscles are not able to pull protein from the blood to increase their size, tone, or strength. The key ingredients for smooth, firm skin tone are enough calories, protein, and exercise.

The amount of protein required in the diet is not large, and most people do not have trouble meeting their needs. An adult female needs 44 grammes of protein each day. The daily allotment can be obtained from a 3-ounce serving of fish, two glasses of milk, and three slices of bread. An adult male needs 56 grammes of protein each day. This requirement can be met by adding 8 ounces of baked beans to the foregoing foods. The average protein intake is closer to 99 grammes. A breakfast of two eggs, toast, bacon, milk, and coffee contains the entire day's allotment of protein. *(Table 1, opposite)*

When more protein is consumed than is needed it does not build more muscles or increase muscle tone; it adds to stress on the body because the extra protein must be broken down and its toxic nitrogen waste excreted in the urine. There is no need to take protein powders or tablets to meet protein needs.

Fats

Dietary fats provide concentrated calories to the body. Three fats called linoleic,

Table 1	Protein Menu	Grammes of Protein
Breakfast:	Low-fat milk (4 fl.oz.)	4.0 grammes
	Whole wheat toast (2 slices)	4.8 grammes
	Orange juice (6 fl.oz.)	0.0 grammes
Lunch:	Turkey (2 oz./50g)	18.5 grammes
	Lettuce	0.0 grammes
	Whole wheat bread (2 slices)	4.8 grammes
	Banana (1 medium)	1.6 grammes
	Low-fat milk (8 fl.oz.)	8.0 grammes
Dinner:	Vegetable stew with beans (average serving)	10.0 grammes
	Fruit salad (1 bowl)	0.0 grammes
	Yoghurt dressing	4.0 grammes
	Total protein	66.7 grammes
	Advised daily allowance (Adult men)	56 grammes
	Advised daily allowance (Adult women)	44 grammes

linolenic, and arachidonic acids are types of polyunsaturated fat. Linoleic acid can be converted in the body to the other two, so it is the only essential fat. Deficiency of linoleic acid results in red, scaly skin areas that resemble eczema. The blotchy areas appear first on the face, clustered near the oil-secreting glands, and then in the folds of the nose and lips, the forehead, the eyes, and the cheeks. Sometimes these dry, rough areas are found on the neck, upper arms, shoulders, and buttocks.

Table 2	Dietary Sources of Linoleic Acid	Linoleic Acid g/tsp
	Safflower oil	15
	Corn oil	12
	Mayonnaise	8
	Peanut oil	7
	Margarine	1–7
	Olive oil	1

A deficiency of these important fats is not common in people who consume a variety of foods such as vegetable oils, vegetables, dried beans and peas, margarine, whole grain breads and cereals, nuts, and seeds. The amount considered necessary for health is only 2% of total calories, or approximately one tablespoon of oil a day. A deficiency of fat has been found in infants fed formulas lacking linoleic acid. The skin sores also are seen in adults maintained for too long on fat-free diets. A combination of linseed oil or linoleic acid combined with vitamin B_6 has been an effective treatment for some fat-related skin problems. *(Table 2, opposite)*

Another important fat called gamma linolenic acid (GLA) might contribute to the health of the skin. The first step in the body to activate linoleic acid is to convert it to GLA. A type of eczema called atopic eczema begins in infancy and childhood and can continue throughout life. This skin condition might be caused by poor conversion of linoleic acid to GLA. Breast-fed infants are protected from atopic eczema because breastmilk contains GLA. Evening primrose oil contains GLA and might improve the symptoms of eczema in some cases.

A diet that contains less than 10% total fat, not just linoleic acid, also can cause dry and flaky skin. Glands embedded within the hair follicle secrete oils that lubricate the hair and give it a sheen. These glands rely on the diet for a supply of fats. When this supply is stopped the hair can become dry and dull. The application of creams containing oils such as linoleic acid does not make up for a poor diet and might mask an underlying nutritional deficiency.

Brittle nails that result from frequent

washing or scrubbing might benefit from a fat-containing moisturiser. The fat helps to seal in water that the nails absorb during soaking.

The B-Complex Vitamins

A deficiency of any B vitamin causes skin and hair changes that range from minor to severe. The B vitamins associated with skin and hair problems are vitamin B_2, niacin, vitamin B_6, folic acid, vitamin B_{12}, pantothenic acid, and biotin.

Vitamin B_2: A deficiency of vitamin B_2 can cause red sores, blisters, and cracks at the corners of the mouth. This condition is called cheilosis. Many other factors can cause cracks and sores at the corners of the mouth, including hot or spicy foods, alcohol, tobacco, chemicals in mouthwashes and toothpastes, and bacteria from food or the environment.

Low levels of vitamin B_2 also might cause the skin to be oily and flaky. Changes in the tongue are another sign of vitamin B_2 deficiency. The tongue becomes glossy, smooth, and purplish or magenta (known as glossitis). These changes are sometimes painful.

Good sources of vitamin B_2 include milk and milk products (yoghurt, cheese, and cottage cheese), mushrooms, broccoli, dark green leafy vegetables, asparagus, avocado, brussels sprouts, and fish. This nutrient is easily destroyed by ultraviolet and flourescent light.

Niacin: Skin problems might be early symptoms of niacin deficiency. If the diet is lacking in this B vitamin, the skin might develop a sunburn-like appearance that disappears and is followed by blotchy spots, first light red in colour, then turning darker red and purple. Swelling might occur, the skin might peel, and sores might develop. In advanced stages of a niacin deficiency, the skin darkens and has severe flaking and sores. Only those areas of the skin exposed to sunlight are affected, such as the hands, forearms, face, and neck. Dermatitis occurs symmetrically on both hands, arms, or feet. The tongue becomes swollen and bright red, and this colour can extend to the lips. Dermatitis is not terribly painful, but burning and itching sensations are present. Sores on the tongue and lips, however, can be quite painful.

A person who consumes a diet low in either niacin or the amino acid tryptophan might develop skin problems. Tryptophan can be converted to niacin in the body so even if inadequate amounts of niacin are present, the body can be adequately nourished if the diet is rich in tryptophan. *(Table 3, page 30)*

Vitamin B$_6$: A vitamin B$_6$ deficiency is characterised by weakness, nervousness, and skin irritations including cracks at the corners of the mouth and redness and itching of the skin. Certain types of eczema and oily dermatitis can be treated effectively with vitamin B$_6$. Some forms of acne and seborrhoea (a chronic inflammation of the sebaceous glands that causes overproduction of oil and skin eruptions) have responded to an increased intake of vitamin B$_6$. Some skin problems have been successfully treated with the vitamin applied in an ointment base as well as with supplements.

Vitamin B$_6$ is important in the formation of red blood cells. A deficiency of this vitamin causes anaemia and its associated symptoms of poor concentration, lethargy, and pale skin.

Although the vitamin is effective in the

treatment of some skin problems, intakes that exceed 500 milligrams (the advised daily allowance is 2 milligrams) might cause toxic symptoms, such as loss of coordination and difficulty walking, numbness and tingling, and nervous system abnormalities. Most of these symptoms are only temporary and disappear if the supplement is discontinued; however, some numbness and tingling might be a sign of permanent nerve damage.

Many people might not consume enough vitamin B_6. Persons likely to be low in this nutrient are those with poor eating habits, the elderly, dieters, pregnant women, nursing mothers, and alcoholics. In addition, individuals consuming high protein diets, or taking steroid drugs or birth control pills, have a higher need for vitamin B_6. This water-soluble nutrient is easily lost when foods are processed, since vitamin B_6 is destroyed by heat, light, and air. The vitamin might be destroyed when foods are cooked or otherwise processed. *(Table 4, page 31)*

Folic Acid: Although a deficiency of folic acid might not cause dermatitis, it can cause anaemia that results in pale skin.

The rosy colour of the skin is partially

Food	Serving Size	Tryptophan Content mg	Niacin Content mg	Total Niacin Content mg
Table 3	**The Niacin Content of Selected Foods**			
Chicken	2 pieces	125	5.8	7.9
Beans, dried	4oz./110g	181	2.1	5.1
Milk	8 fl.oz.	113	0.2	2.1
Egg	1 large	97	0.03	1.63
Banana	1 medium	31	0.8	1.3
Bread	1 slice	23	0.6	1.0
Orange	1 medium	5	0.5	0.6
Carrot	1 medium	8	0.4	0.5
Green beans	4oz./110g	17	0.2	0.5

Advised daily allowance for Adults –
Men: 18 mg   Women: 15 mg

caused by the red blood moving through blood vessels within and below the surface of the skin. When a person is anaemic, the number of red blood cells in the blood is reduced. This causes the blood to be pale, rather than bright red, and less able to provide the underlying colour to skin. In addition, red blood cells are the components of blood that carry oxygen to all the tissues. Folic acid deficiency reduces the amount of oxygen available to the cells of the skin, hair, and nails. Lack of oxygen reduces the cells' ability to perform normal

Table 4	Vitamin B_6 Content of Selected Foods	
Food	**Serving Size**	**B_6 Content mg/ Serving**
Banana	1 medium	480
Avocado	1/2 medium	420
Hamburger, 21% fat, cooked	3oz./80g	391
Chicken	3oz./80g	340
Halibut	3oz./80g	289
Potato	1 medium	200
Spinach, cooked	4oz./110g	161
Rice, brown, cooked	3oz./80g	127
Peas, green	3oz./80g	110
Walnuts	8–10 halves	109
Broccoli, cooked	4oz./110g	107
Milk	8 fl.oz.	98
Frankfurter	2	98
Orange	1 medium	90
Melon	1/4 melon	90
Tomato	1/2 medium	74
Wheat Germ	1 tbsp	55
Egg	1 medium	49
Cottage Cheese	4oz./110g	46
Apple	1 medium	45
Bread, whole wheat	1 slice	41
Rice, white, enriched, cooked	3oz./80g	30
Bread, white, enriched	1 slice	9
Oils, Fats, Margarine, Butter	1 tbsp	0

Advised daily allowance for Adults –
Men: 2.2 mg   Women: 2.0 mg

metabolic functions and the health of the tissues suffers.

Children who consume a diet low in folic acid develop skin eruptions similar to chicken pox or measles. Children are more susceptible to these skin changes because their cells are broken down and replaced more quickly than adults. Folic acid also is required for the development of all new cells in the body. The increased need to manufacture skin cells in the growing child depletes supplies of the vitamin and skin problems might result. The tongue is another part of the body where new cells are formed daily. When the diet is low in folic acid the tongue becomes smooth and glossy.

The average diet might be low in folic acid. When diets are analysed, the folic acid content averages 227 mcg/day or about one-half of the advised daily intake. To help meet folic acid needs, at least one serving (4oz./110g cooked or 8oz./220g raw) of dark green leafy vegetables should be included in the diet each day. *(Table 5, page 34)*

Folic acid can be lost during storage, processing, cooking, and reheating of foods. Foods should be purchased fresh and stored and cooked for a short time. Only the amount that can be eaten at one time should be prepared. Reheating folic acid-rich foods can deplete most of the vitamin.

Vitamin B_{12}: Vitamin B_{12} is closely related to folic acid in the maintenance of healthy blood and tissues. Anaemia, with its associated pallor of the skin, develops if vitamin B_{12} status is poor. In addition, vitamin B_{12} and folic acid are important in the production of new cells and tissues. As skin and hair cells slough off and as nails grow they require continual manufacture of new cells that would not occur without ample amounts of vitamin B_{12} and folic acid in the diet. The result might be slow growth of hair and nails, hair loss, and abnormalities of the skin.

A deficiency of either vitamin B_{12} or folic acid might cause loss of appetite, which would further reduce food and nutrient intake and increase a person's risk of malnutrition. A lack of vitamin B_{12} might cause greying of hair; however, taking supplements when no deficiency exists does not prevent greying.

Vitamin B_{12} is found only in foods from animal sources. Strict vegetarians who do

Table 5	Folic Acid Content of Selected Foods	
Food	Serving Size	Folic Acid mcg/Serving
Yeast, brewer's	1 tbsp	313
Spinach, raw	4oz./110g	106
Orange juice, fresh or frozen, reconstituted	6 fl.oz.	102
Lettuce, romaine	3oz./80g	98
Spinach, cooked	4oz./110g	82
Broccoli, cooked	4oz./110g	44
Lettuce, head or leaf	3oz./80g	20
Bread, whole wheat	1 slice	16
Bread, white	1 slice	10
Mushrooms, raw	2oz./50g	8

not consume meat, poultry, fish, eggs, or low-fat dairy foods might not consume adequate amounts of this vitamin to meet daily needs. Children and pregnant women who are strict vegetarians, and infants nursed by strict vegetarian mothers, are at risk of deficiencies. The elderly are also at risk of deficiency of vitamin B_{12}. Unlike other water-soluble B vitamins that are easily lost in the urine, vitamin B_{12} is stored in the body. If dietary intake was adequate during a period of a person's life, it would take months or years to develop a deficiency of the vitamin. However, to avoid anaemia and irreversible nerve damage that can develop, a vitamin B_{12} supplement should be taken when no dietary source of the vitamin is included in the diet. Vegetarians who consume milk, milk products, or eggs are not at risk of a deficiency, since all these foods contain vitamin B_{12}.

The amount of foods from animal sources needed to obtain enough vitamin B_{12} is not large. The advised daily allowance for vitamin B_{12} is 3 micrograms for adults. This amount can be obained from three servings (2 to 3 ounces of meat or 1 cup milk or yoghurt) of protein foods from animal sources such as beef, pork, lamb, chicken, fish, turkey, and low-fat dairy foods.

Pantothenic Acid: Consumption of a diet that is inadequate in pantothenic acid can leave the skin dry and flaky. A burning sensation on the bottoms of the feet is also a sign of deficiency. In addition, this B vitamin is important in the normal growth and colour of hair.

Pantothenic acid is found in all types of food from meat and chicken to whole grain breads, cereals, and vegetables.

Significant amounts of pantothenic acid are lost during the milling and refining of processed grains. As much as 75% of the amount present in food is lost during tinning, freezing, and refining. People who eat a diet high in processed foods can develop a deficiency of pantothenic acid. *(Table 6, below)* Pantothenic acid intake can be increased by consuming whole wheat bread and brown rice rather than white bread and white rice, fresh fruits and vegetables, dried beans and peas, lean meats, fish and poultry, and low-fat milk and milk products.

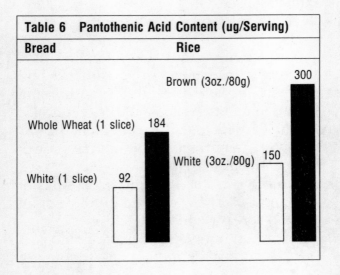

Table 6	Pantothenic Acid Content (ug/Serving)	
Bread	**Rice**	

Brown (3oz./80g) 300

Whole Wheat (1 slice) 184

White (3oz./80g) 150

White (1 slice) 92

Biotin: Biotin deficiency symptoms include hair loss, premature wrinkles, and a scaly skin rash. A deficiency is uncommon, however, because biotin is formed by bacteria found naturally in the intestinal tract.

A protein in raw egg whites called avidin can bind to biotin in the intestines and prevent it from being absorbed. Consumption of several raw eggs a day might cause a biotin deficiency. Avidin is destroyed by high temperatures and eggs that are cooked do not inhibit absorption of the B vitamin.

A biotin deficiency is more likely to occur in pregnant women, alcoholics, the elderly, and athletes. Prolonged diarrhoea also might cause biotin deficiency. Some medications, such as antibiotics, destroy the important bacteria that produce the vitamin and a deficiency can develop.

Foods from both plant and animal sources contain biotin. The richest sources are offal meats, milk, dried beans and peas, whole grain breads and cereals, and nuts.

Vitamin C

The oil-producing glands in the follicle of the hair shaft do not produce adequate amounts of oils without vitamin C. A lack of this vitamin causes the hair to break or split easily. If the hair breaks off just under the surface of the skin a new hair growing in the follicle can be cramped, and either coil into an abnormal circular pattern or form imperfectly. The hair becomes dry, kinky, and tangles or splits.

Vitamin C is needed for the formation of collagen, the glue that holds together the cells of the skin and other tissues. Collagen provides the framework on which blood vessels are supported. Without adequate amounts of vitamin C, collagen is not formed properly. Weak collagen causes the small blood vessels to tear, a condition that shows up as tiny, pinpoint spots below the skin; they can be red, violet, brown, or yellow. Bruises occur more easily. Pliable, soft skin loses its elasticity and cuts and scratches take longer to heal. Gums are prone to bleeding when the diet does not supply enough vitamin C.

People who take aspirin often or are

under stress, women using oral contraceptives, and people who drink alcohol or smoke cigarettes might need more vitamin C each day than is recommended by the advised daily allowance.

Vitamin C is not stored in the body and requirements must be met daily from the diet. Vitamin C is easily lost when foods are stored for extended periods of time, are cooked in water and the water is thrown away, are reheated, are heated and kept warm such as in cafeteria lines, or are not stored at cold temperatures. Vitamin C-rich foods such as fruits and vegetables should be purchased fresh or frozen, immediately stored at temperatures below 40 degrees, and cooked for a minimal amount of time in a small amount of water. Any water used in cooking should be used in gravies, sauces, stews, or soups.

The Fat-Soluble Vitamins

The fat-soluble vitamins related to the health of hair, skin, and nails include vitamin A and vitamin E. These vitamins are stored in the body, and excesses are not excreted in the urine as are excesses of water-soluble vitamins. Deficiency symptoms develop slowly because fat-soluble vitamins can be stored and used over time. Because fat-soluble vitamins are not excreted, they can build up in the body and reach toxic levels.

Vitamin A: Vitamin A is important in the maintenance of healthy skin. Without adequate amounts of this vitamin, the soft, smooth surface of the skin becomes scaly and dry. Although this condition can result from several nutrient deficiencies, the dryness and flakiness in a vitamin A deficiency is partially caused by the breakdown of the sweat glands that normally keep skin moist. The scalp can become reddened and sore and the hair can become dry and bleached out. Hair loss and dandruff are other signs of a vitamin A deficiency.

Like the essential fats and vitamin C, a lack of vitamin A is associated with small hard bumps on the skin. Vitamin A is necessary for healthy oil production in the skin and scalp. Adequate intake of vitamin A helps to maintain healthy, shiny, hair and moist skin that is not prone to premature wrinkles.

Dieters, women, teenagers, children,

some minorities, and the elderly often eat diets that are deficient in vitamin A.

To increase the daily intake of vitamin A a person should consume four or more servings of fruits and vegetables. Deep orange and yellow fruits and vegetables are good sources. The vitamin A content of fruit and vegetables varies depending on the intensity of the plant's colour; a pale apricot contains less vitamin A than a dark apricot. *(Table 7, page 42)*

The advised daily allowance for vitamin A is 5,000 IU's for adult males and 4,000 IU's for adult females. Doses exceeding 25,000 IU consumed over long periods of time can be toxic. Symptoms of a vitamin A toxicity include dry rough skin, fingernails that are brittle and crack or peel, and hair that breaks and falls out.

The vitamin A in plant foods is called the carotenoids. Beta carotene is the most common carotenoid. Regardless of the dose, the only adverse side effect of taking large doses of this form of vitamin A is a yellowing of the skin, primarily on the palms and soles of the feet. This discolouration disappears when the consumption of carotene is reduced.

Table 7 Vitamin A Content of Selected Foods		
Food	Serving Size	Vitamin A Content per Serving
Canteloupe, with rind (5″ diam.)	1/2 melon	9,240
Carrots, cooked, drained	3oz./80g	8,140
Spinach, cooked drained	4oz./110g	7,290
Broccoli, cooked, drained	5oz./135g	3,205
Apricots, tinned in syrup	4oz./110g	2,245
Tomatoes, tinned	6oz./160g	2,170
Lettuce, romaine	3oz./80g	1,050
Green peas, tinned	3oz./80g	585
Orange juice, from concentrate	6 fl.oz.	410

Advised daily allowance –
Men: 5,000 IU's   Women: 4,000 IU's

Vitamin E: Vitamin E protects both vitamin A and the polyunsaturated fats in the body and is important for moist skin. Vitamin E might prevent premature aging of the skin. This fat-soluble vitamin prevents the accumulation of pigment that forms brown spots on the skin as people get older. Years of exposure to sunshine and biological changes cause these spots. The brown pigment is produced by specialised cells in the skin that increase in number with age.

When vitamin E is added to sunscreen

lotions it protects the skin from damage caused by ultraviolet light. It reduces both burning of the outer layers of the skin and damage to deeper cells. The lotion should contain other agents, besides vitamin E, that protect the skin from sun (such as PABA) to increase the effectiveness of the sunscreen.

Vitamin E is an antioxidant that protects cells from destruction by oxygen and other reactive compounds called free radicals. Free radicals are produced by cigarette smoke, air pollution, incomplete breakdown of proteins and fats in the body, and by other substances in the environment. One theory is that the long-term accumulation of waste from free radicals and the destruction of cell membranes might contribute to premature aging. *(Graph 1, page 44)*

Cold pressed vegetable oils, whole grain breads and cereals, green leafy vegetables, wheat germ, and dried beans and peas are rich sources of this vitamin. Refined flour and breads, processed vegetable oils, and other refined foods are not reliable sources of vitamin E.

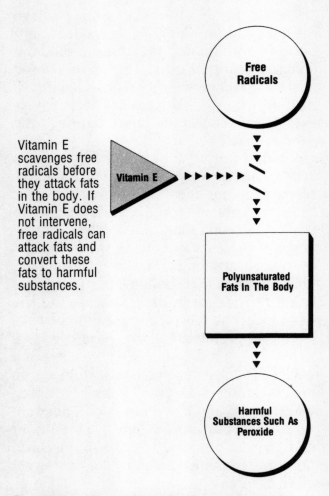

Vitamin E scavenges free radicals before they attack fats in the body. If Vitamin E does not intervene, free radicals can attack fats and convert these fats to harmful substances.

Free Radicals

Vitamin E

Polyunsaturated Fats In The Body

Harmful Substances Such As Peroxide

Graph 1:   How Vitamin E protects cells

The Minerals

Minerals are found in body tissues and help regulate thousands of body processes. In addition, many vitamins cannot function without the assistance of minerals. The minerals that have a specific influence on the health of hair, skin, or nails include copper, iron, and zinc.

Copper: Copper is found in every tissue and is involved in many processes in the body. It is important in the formation of red blood cells. A deficiency of copper causes anaemia, weakness, lethargy, poor concentration, and pale skin.

Copper is necessary for the normal formation of connective tissue in all tissues, including the skin. Connective tissue is malformed when there is a copper deficiency, which might result in improper wound healing, small red blotches under the skin from the rupture of blood vessels, and skin that bruises easily.

Copper is important in the formation of skin pigment (melanin) and maintenance of healthy colour in skin. When the diet is inadequate in copper the skin might be pale and blotchy.

A copper deficiency also is associated

with colour changes or loss of colour from the hair.

The advised daily allowance for copper is 2 mg to 3 mg each day. A diet that contains several servings of copper-rich foods such as whole grain breads and cereals, shell-fish, nuts, offal meats, chicken, dried beans and peas, and dark green leafy vegetables will probably meet the daily recommendations for this mineral. If the diet is comprised of refined flours, grains, breads, and convenience and processed foods, copper intake might not be adequate to maintain the health of skin and hair.

Iron: An iron-poor diet can affect the nails. Brittle, fragile, and dull nails or nails with ridges can be a result of poor iron intake. In a long-term deficiency the nails can become spoon-shaped. When this happens the nail either flattens out or curves abnormally. Other signs of poor iron status are a smooth red tongue, a suppressed immune system, and frequent colds or infections. The most well-known symptom of iron deficiency is anaemia. This disorder can result in pale skin. *(Figure 4, page 48)*

Iron deficiency is a common form of malnutrition found in the West. Those people at risk include pre-menopausal women, the elderly, adolescents, infants, and children. Low-income groups, the old, and adolescents consume a limited variety of foods, have a reduced food intake, or have social or economic factors that interfere with daily food intake of iron-rich foods.

Iron is found in lean meat, dried beans and peas, dark green leafy vegetables, dried fruits, and grains. Iron in foods from animal sources is absorbed more easily by the body than iron in foods from plant sources. The iron in vegetables and grains is better absorbed if consumed with a food high in vitamin C. The iron content of the diet can also be increased by cooking foods in cast iron pots, combining iron-rich foods from plant sources with iron-rich foods from animal sources, and consuming several iron-rich foods daily.

Zinc: Zinc is one of the healing components of calamine lotion and was first used as a treatment for skin problems.

Zinc aids in the formation of collagen. Without this essential connective tissue, cells of the skin would pull away from each other, blood would leak out of blood vessels, and the skin would "come unglued."

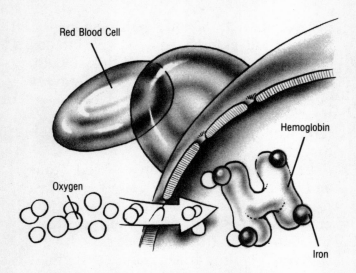

Figure 4: Iron in Red Blood Cells

The iron in red blood cells is attached to the protein haemoglobin. Oxygen from the lungs binds to the iron and is carried to all tissues in the body.

Skin on the abdomen, thighs, hips, and breasts can be scarred by "stretch marks" caused by breaks in the connective tissue and other elastic-like fibres (elastin) in the skin. Zinc and copper are necessary for the normal formation and cross-linking of these support tissues. A deficiency of these minerals would cause malformation of the connective tissue and elastin fibres and might increase the likelihood that these fibres would break when stretched, causing stretch marks.

Zinc is necessary for the formation of new protein around a cut, scrape, or burn. Consumption of a diet that is even marginally deficient in zinc results in impaired wound healing and skin that is dry and rough. Cuts, scrapes, and burns heal slowly. Increased hair loss and baldness also are possible with a zinc deficiency. Some skin disorders, such as eczema, might respond to an increase in dietary zinc.

Zinc affects the health of skin and hair in another way: it is needed in the production of the protein that carries vitamin A through the blood. Zinc releases vitamin A from its storage sites in the liver and regulates the amount of vitamin A that circulates in the blood and is available to the tissues. Without zinc, a deficiency of vitamin A occurs even though intake and body stores of the vitamin appear adequate. This interaction with vitamin A is one of the reasons zinc has been used in the treatment of acne. Zinc is also involved in the regulation of normal oil secretion from the skin. Since acne is caused by oversecretion of oils from the sebaceous glands, zinc might normalise this condition.

Zinc is essential to the normal colour of nails. A zinc deficiency might cause white spots to form on the fingernails. Large spots remain and must grow out with the nail; this process can take five to six months. Fasting or short-term restrictive diets might encourage a zinc deficiency. Nails that are pale, rather than pink, might be a sign of low zinc and low vitamin B_6.

The average diet contains about 10 mg to 15 mg of zinc. Zinc deficiency might be common, particularly among preschool children, pregnant women, the elderly, people with low incomes, and people who suffer from severe stress from burns, injury, and surgery. Athletes and strict vegetarians (those who consume no meat, chicken, or fish) also might consume inadequate amounts of absorbable zinc. Daily sources of zinc are necessary during periods of wound healing since cuts and scrapes draw zinc from surrounding areas of the body and the stress of wound healing can deplete body stores of the mineral.

Factors that contribute to poor zinc status include low meat consumption; increased consumption of refined cereals, breads, and other grain products; reliance on convenience foods; and a diet high in sugar and fat. Zinc absorption is reduced when large amounts of calcium are consumed. Zinc is also poorly absorbed when the diet is too high in fibre. Fibre binds to zinc in the intestines and carries the mineral out of the body. Although the body stores zinc, these stores are not easily retrieved in times of need and a daily dietary source of the mineral is necessary to maintain normal body processes.

Good sources of zinc include seafood, oysters, meats, milk, and whole grain bread and cereal. The zinc in foods from animal sources is absorbed more readily than that in vegetables and grains.

Water

One nutrient often forgotten, but vitally important for the skin, hair, and nails, is water. Cells that contain adequate amounts of water keep the skin moist and fresh-looking. Water is the main component of perspiration, which is important in keeping skin moisturised. During exercise, perspiration stimulates the oil-producing glands of the hair follicles to secrete oils that keep the hair moisturised.

A person needs 6 to 8 glasses of fluid a day to maintain the proper fluid balance in the body; more is needed if a person exercises or perspires heavily. To replenish fluids and maintain moist skin, consume several glasses a day of fresh or bottled water, fruit or vegetable juices, decaffeinated tea, or sparkling water. Some other suggestions include fruit juice mixed with sparkling water, or herbal teas. Caffeine in coffee, teas, and some cola drinks and alcohol have a diuretic action on the body and cause the cells of the skin and other tissues to lose water. These drinks might have a drying effect on the skin.

3

Coping with the Elements: Wind, Cold, and Sun

Dry indoor air, the cold winds of winter, and the hot sun of summer take their toll on skin and hair.

In the wintertime, the humidity in the air drops, and skin becomes dry and rough. Cold winds chap and dry the skin and draw moisture from the hair. These effects can be counteracted by a diet that contains adequate amounts of fat-soluble vitamins, minerals, essential fats, and water. Exercise can promote perspiration and keep the skin moist by stimulating the oil-producing glands.

The ultraviolet rays of the sun can age and wrinkle the skin. Collagen, the connective tissue that holds skin cells together, breaks and the elastic fibres in the skin thicken as a result of excessive exposure to the sun. A dark glowing tan may be fashionable, but it affects the health of skin

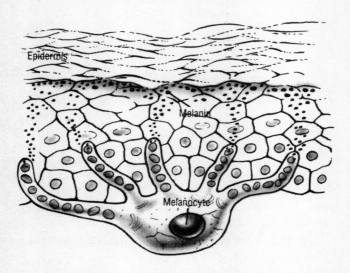

Figure 5: The Skin Darkens in the Presence of Sunlight

Melanocytes release melanin in the presence of sunlight. This pigment migrates to the surface of the skin and the tan that results protects the body from further sun damage.

and hair and increases the risk of cancer. *(Figure 5, above)*

Cell membranes are an important line of defence in the body. Cell membranes determine what compounds will and will not enter into the cell. Cancer-causing substances are kept out of the cell by this membrane. Free radicals (see page 85) can destroy the fats that make up the membrane. Nutrients that act as antioxidants protect these delicate cell membranes from destruction by oxidising agents, and so have a role in prevention of skin cancer. Vitamin E, vitamin C, and the mineral selenium all function as antioxidants.

The hot rays of the sun can deplete skin and hair of their natural oil coatings. The skin can flake and become dull and the hair can become brittle and dry. A towel wrapped around the hair provides protection against the drying effects of the sun. Use of moisturisers, adequate intake of the fat-soluble vitamins A and E, and water might counteract the damage caused by sunlight.

4

Lifestyle Factors that Affect the Nourishment of the Skin, Hair, and Nails

Exercise

Physical activity, whether it is planned exercise such as biking or jogging, or normal activity such as washing the car or gardening, stimulates perspiration and the oil-secreting action of the skin. The natural oils help the skin, hair, and nails retain moisture and health. Physical activity increases circulation and is one of the best ways to give the skin a fresh, healthy "glow."

Exercise can increase the need for several nutrients related to health of skin, hair and nails. The most important nutrient to replace during and after exercise is water. More fluids must be consumed to compensate for fluid losses in perspiration. Because thirst is not a good indicator of fluid losses, a person may not drink enough water to replace losses after an exercise session. If exercise is carried out on a hot or humid day, even greater fluid losses are likely to occur. In general, drink twice the amount of fluid it takes to quench thirst to replenish lost fluids.

A person who exercises often can consume more calories to maintain body weight than the sedentary person because of the increased energy burned during physical fitness. The body needs vitamin B_1, vitamin B_2, niacin, pantothenic acid, biotin, and vitamin B_6 to process the additional calories. Whole and unrefined complex carbohydrate foods contain the B vitamins and other trace minerals that are needed for the processing of calories. Refined white flours, breads, and rice might contain adequate quantities of vitamin B_1, vitamin B_2, and niacin, but contain less of the other nutrients than whole grain varieties. These B vitamins also are necessary for healthy skin, hair, and nails. *(Table 8, page 58)*

Increased urinary excretion and decreased circulating levels of zinc are associated with vigorous activity. Low levels of zinc in the body might cause the skin to become dry and rough and the

Table 8 A Comparison of Whole Wheat and "Enriched" White Bread	
Dietary Constituent	Nutrient Content of White Bread as Percent of Whole Wheat Bread (%)
Folacin	63%
Copper	42%
Zinc	38%
Chromium	28%
Dietary Fibre/Mgn	22%
Vitamin B_6	18%
Manganese	12%
Vitamin E	4%

hair to become dull. During periods of strenuous activity, the diet should contain several servings of zinc-rich foods each day. (See page 51 for sources of zinc in the diet.)

During exercise, additional amounts of vitamin E might be needed to protect cell membranes from destruction from oxidising agents. Because exercise increases respiration and oxygen intake, there is a greater chance that oxidising agents will enter the body or be formed during exercise. This nutrient might prevent premature development of brown aging spots.

Dieting

Crash diets and severe restriction of calories do not contribute to healthy skin, hair, and nails. Extreme calorie restriction can cause loss of muscles, poor muscle tone, skin that has lost its tone and firmness, and dry and dull hair. It also can cause skin, hair, and nail problems associated with multiple deficiencies of vitamins and minerals. If intake of polyunsaturated fats is low, dry, red patches might develop on the skin.

Intakes of vitamin B_6, niacin, vitamin B_2, folic acid, biotin, zinc, and iron are all likely to be low in diets containing less than 1,200 calories. These nutrients are necessary for healthy skin, hair and nails. For example, deficiencies of folic acid, vitamin B_{12}, copper, vitamin B_6, and iron result in anaemia and pale skin. Deficiencies of vitamin B_2, zinc, vitamin B_6, and niacin result in rough, dry, red skin patches, or scaly, oily types of dermatitis, and dull, brittle hair.

A weight control diet must provide adequate amounts of all the vitamins and minerals to be an effective, healthy means of losing and maintaining weight loss while also maintaining the health of hair, skin, and nails.

Medications

Many medications have a detrimental effect on nutrient status in the body and can cause problems with skin, hair, and nails. Some prescription and non-prescription medications can interfere with the absorption of vitamins and minerals, increase nutrient excretion, alter how a nutrient is used in the body, or affect the body's ability to store a nutrient. Other medications can affect food intake by altering the taste of food or cause nausea and vomiting.

Alcohol

Alcohol abuse can alter nutritional status and the health of the hair, skin, and nails in several ways. Alcohol reduces the absorption of nutrients, increases nutrient excretion, alters how nutrients are used or stored in the body, and often replaces nutritious foods in the diet and limits nutrient intake. In addition, alcohol increases the rupture of blood vessels under the skin.

Vitamins at risk of depletion during alcohol abuse include folic acid, vitamin B_1, vitamin B_2, niacin, vitamin C, vitamin B_6, and vitamin B_{12}. Minerals depleted during alcohol intake include magnesium and zinc. The results of these losses include dry, flaky skin; dull, dry hair; brittle nails; and anaemia.

The normal production of protein in the body is altered, which can affect the formation of skin and hair. Poor dietary intake of protein and essential fats can result in sparse, dry, or brittle hair and flaky, dry skin.

A skin rash associated with niacin deficiency is found in alcoholics and reflects the reduced absorption and altered use of the B vitamin.

Alcohol has a diuretic effect on the kidneys because the toxic waste products produced by alcohol are broken down and must be excreted. When these waste products are lost so are excesses of water and water-soluble nutrients such as zinc, magnesium, and potassium. Chronic low intake and increased urinary loss of these nutrients can cause rough, dry, or reddened skin. *(Table 9, below)*

Alcohol interferes with the conversion of the essential fat linoleic acid to gamma linolenic acid (GLA). This alteration in the body's ability to use linoleic acid might contribute to some forms of eczema. In some cases, atopic eczema does respond to increased dietary intake of essential fats such as GLA.

Table 9	Nutrient Deficiencies Common in Alcoholism	
	1. Vitamin Depletion	2. Mineral Depletion
	Folic Acid	Magnesium
	Thiamin	Zinc
	Riboflavin	
	Niacin	
	Ascorbic Acid	
	Vitamin B_6	
	Vitamin B_{12}	

Cigarette Smoking

Smoking affects the appearance and health of the skin. Smoking causes constriction of the blood vessels that supply the skin with oxygen and nutrients and remove toxic waste products. When blood vessels are constricted, the blood supply is reduced and the cell's ability to remove waste is reduced. A reduced blood flow can cause the skin to pale and age.

Smoking reduces the body's ability to mend cuts and other wounds. Nicotine causes the blood vessels to spasm and constrict, which impairs blood flow to the damaged area. Without adequate amounts of nutrients and materials carried in the blood, the skin near the incisions dies, cells slough off, and a crusty scab forms that does not heal properly.

Smoking increases vitamin C requirements by approximately 40 to 80 milligrams. Adequate amounts of vitamin C are needed to maintain the firmness and tone of the skin and to prevent broken blood vessels and tiny haemorrhages below the surface of the skin.

5

Special Problems of the Skin

Acne

Several factors make for the development of this skin disorder including genetics, bacterial growth on a person's skin, emotional stress, some cosmetics, changes in climate or environmental circumstances, and diet.

Acne begins in the hair follicle and its accompanying sebaceous glands. Normally, the pores of the skin secrete their oils from the hair follicle up through the opening to the skin's surface. Dead cells produced by the follicle are carried to the skin's surface and washed or wiped away. In acne, dead cells and other debris stick to the follicle and the oils in the hair follicle mix with the dead cells. This forms a plug that is pushed to the surface of the skin, and stretches and weakens the opening of the hair duct and blocks removal of cellular debris and oils. Bacteria that live in the hair follicle convert the sebum and dead cells into compounds that irritate the lining of the follicle and eventually the follicle ruptures. Sebum and acids are released into the surrounding dermis, which causes inflammation and damage to the skin. *(Figure 6, page 66)*

The primary aid in the prevention and treatment of acne is to keep the skin clean and oil-free. Some antibiotic medications, such as tetracycline, limit the growth of bacteria in the hair follicle and are effective in the treatment of acne for some people. Oestrogen is used in the treatment of acne in some females. A synthetic form of vitamin A called retinoic acid (available by prescription) and benzoyl peroxide might help prevent the formation or release the plug of sebum that forms in acne or reduce the formation of sebum.

Zinc might also be effective in the treatment of acne. Some people show fewer skin sores and their skin is less oily after supplementation with zinc sulphate. A zinc deficiency might increase the symptoms of acne.

None of the foods commonly thought to

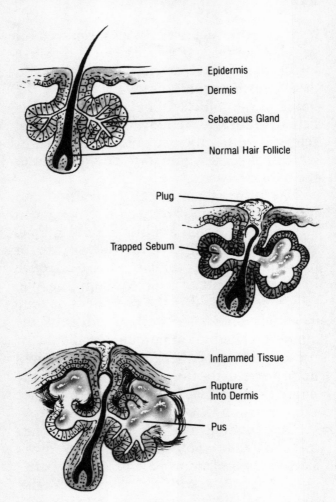

Figure 6:   How acne develops

cause acne in teenagers, such as chocolate, soft drinks, sugar, greasy foods, nuts, milk, salt or iodine, appear to be linked to the skin disorder. The stress of adolescence and its effect on stress hormones affect the condition, in which case the cure is simple but does require patience.

The research on diet and acne is limited, however a nutritious diet will probably provide the nutrients that will aid a person in the prevention and treatment of acne.

Aging

The experiences of life are recorded on the skin. Skin is a soft, smooth surface in youth and over the years it accumulates the lines of a thousand smiles and frowns. Skin tone declines with increasing age. Connective tissue deteriorates, the skin sags, and wrinkles form. The female hormone oestrogen protects against premature aging, but when levels of this hormone decline after menopause, the skin will lose suppleness. The "weathering" from exposure to sun and wind also can affect the skin. Good nutrition is an important component in preventing of unnecessary aging of the skin.

Skin cells die and are replaced faster than most body cells, so new supplies of nutrients are constantly needed to keep skin healthy and looking youthful. Healthy blood with ample red blood cells is vital to maintain a constant supply of nutrients to the skin, hair, and nails. All of the nutrients required for blood formation, such as copper, iron, folic acid, vitamin B_{12}, vitamin C, vitamin B_6, zinc, vitamin E, pantothenic acid, and protein, must be supplied in adequate amounts in the daily diet.

Vitamin E is important in the prevention of premature aging and wrinkling of skin. It is an antioxidant and protects the skin from substances in the air and environment that promote aging. Vitamin E helps prevent brown age spots, commonly seen on the backs of the hands, arms, and shoulders. This vitamin also protects the polyunsaturated fats in cell membranes from destruction so that cells in the skin, hair, and nails remain healthy. Biotin and vitamin A also are important to prevent premature aging of the skin.

Some elderly people have diets that lack

nutrients important to skin, hair, and nails. Protein foods supply nutrients needed to replace dead cells. Two servings of protein foods each day help maintain adequate protein intake. Protein foods include lean meats, poultry, fish, dried beans, dried peas, cheese, and milk.

Burns

The body requires all the vitamins and minerals to heal burns. However, zinc, vitamin C, vitamin A, folic acid, vitamin B_{12}, and vitamin E are especially important in the recovery from burns.

Bruises

Bruises are a sign that blood vessels under the skin have broken. To repair these blood vessels and speed the healing of the skin, protein, zinc, vitamin C, vitamin A, copper, calcium, vitamin E, folic acid, vitamin B_{12}, and other B vitamins are all necessary. If the diet provides these vitamins and minerals and bruising or bleeding still continues, consult a doctor.

Chronic consumption of alcohol or the continued smoking of cigarettes depletes the body of some nutrients and can interfere with the healing of wounds and bruises.

Dry Skin And Dandruff

Skin becomes dry because it lacks moisture from within or because substances that normally retain moisture are lacking. The skin cells need water and this nutrient is continually lost from the surface of the skin. Water loss is greatest during winter when cold winds, low humidity, and dry indoor heating increases evaporation from the skin.

Coffee, black tea, and alcoholic beverages contain diuretics that move water out of the cells and encourage water loss and dryness. These beverages should not be included in the recommended 6 to 8 glasses of fluids consumed each day.

People who are physically active need more water to replace losses from perspiration. Perspiring promotes moist skin by stimulating tiny glands that keep the skin coated with natural oils. Regular physical activity and drinking water maintain moist, healthy skin.

Fat in the diet is another important nutrient for moist skin. The polyunsaturated fats in vegetable oils contribute to the natural oils of the skin. Women and teenage girls who are on strict diets might not consume enough fat. Older adults who live on a low calorie diet might not consume ample amounts of fat in the diet. If the diet is very low in fat, add a tablespoon of vegetable oil to the daily salad. Safflower and sunflower oils are the best sources of polyunsaturated oils. Soy and corn oils also are good choices. Nuts, seeds, soft margarines, and avocado provide good sources of fat. These fatty foods are only to be advised for those people who consume less than 15% of their calories as fat. Chronic or severe dieting, cigarettes, and alcohol can increase the likelihood for nutrient deficiencies and might result in dry skin or dandruff.

The fat-soluble vitamins A and E are not absorbed unless some fat is available in the diet. These nutrients are essential for healthy, moist skin. If the skin becomes dry at a particular time of the year, such as in the winter, foods high in vitamins A and E should be increased to at least two servings a day. (Pages 42–43 for dietary sources of vitamins A and E.)

The water-soluble vitamins also are important to maintain moist, subtle skin. These include vitamin B_1, vitamin B_2, niacin, pantothenic acid, vitamin B_6, folic acid, vitamin B_{12}, and biotin. Vitamin C helps the oil-secreting glands function properly. Without enough vitamin C, the skin does not make adequate amounts of the natural oil coating of the skin to keep the skin from drying out. Since many factors increase the need for vitamin C, such as smoking, oral contraceptives, and stress, include two or more servings a day of vitamin C-rich foods in the diet. (See page 39 for dietary sources of vitamin C.)

Eczema

Eczema is a general term for chronic skin inflammation and irritation that can be caused by several factors including an allergic reaction to pollens, dust, the sun, dry air, or other environmental factors. Symptoms of eczema might be accelerated by stress and anxiety. If the condition is localised on the face it might be caused by cosmetics. If the skin disorder is only on the hands it might be caused by exposure to chemical irritants. Eczema is also called atopic dermatitis, atopic eczema, or eczematous dermatitis. The skin is red with blisters and scales. Damaged areas of the skin harden and darken. An individual with eczema often suffers itching and the skin might burn or ache and red rashes or dry spots can develop.

A deficiency of linoleic acid produces eczematous patches on the skin, as does inadequate vitamin B_2, biotin, vitamin B_6, pantothenic acid, vitamin A, and zinc. However, inclusion of these nutrients in the diet will help only if the eczema is caused by a nutrient deficiency.

When food allergies are the cause, appropriate steps can be taken to eliminate the offending foods. Foods that most often cause allergic reactions include wheat, corn, milk, chocolate, oranges, nuts, strawberries and shellfish.

Hair Loss

Although other lifestyle factors, such as stress, genetics, and age, contribute to hair loss, some nutrients are related to the maintenance of healthy hair. The B vitamins, such as biotin, are important for the maintenance of hair. A deficiency of vitamin A can cause the hair to be dry; vitamin C deficiency causes the hair to split, tangle, and break; and a copper deficiency causes kinky hair and loss of colour.

Herpes

The treatment of viral infections such as herpes includes maintaining a healthy immune system. Nutrients involved in the immune system include zinc, vitamin C, vitamin A, and protein. Nutrients that help repair damaged tissues as are seen in the herpes blisters include folic acid, vitamin B_{12}, zinc, vitamin C, vitamin A, and protein. The amino acid lysine might reduce both the severity and frequency of herpes infections.

Itching

Skin that itches might be caused by either dry skin (see section on Dry Skin And Dandruff) or an allergic reaction to environmental factors such as dust, plants, pets, or clothing. Itching also might be caused by ingested substances such as food, beverages, or medications. Another cause of chronic itching might be iron deficiency. Some people who suffer from itchy skin respond to an increase in dietary or supplemental iron. Iron-deficiency can reduce the oxygen supply to the skin, scalp, and other tissues and cause changes in the skin that might result in itching or flaking. The deficiency might not be low enough to cause anaemia. Niacin, vitamin B_6, and zinc might help prevent itchy skin. Chronic use of cigarettes and alcohol might cause nutrient deficiencies and dry, itchy skin.

Nails

The health of the nails depends on nutrition. brittle, fragile nails with ridges might be a sign of iron deficiency. A zinc deficiency might cause white spots to appear on the nail. All nutrients related to healthy blood are required to supply the nails with a constant supply of nutrients and oxygen.

Psoriasis

Psoriasis is a chronic, inflammatory skin condition that is characterised by dry, red skin patches covered with silvery white scales and with bleeding points underneath the sores. The condition might come and go, but it is often chronic.

A diet free from fat and low in protein might alleviate the symptoms of psoriasis, but people have difficulty complying with this strict diet and the symptoms return when old diet habits are resumed. Some evidence indicates that a diet low in tryptophan (an amino acid) reduces the severity of the symptoms.

Psoriasis can be triggered by stressful events, and some success is reported from using biofeedback therapy, relaxation techniques, and psychotherapy in lessening the disease.

Sunburn

The best protection against sunburn is to avoid excess exposure to the sun's rays. Repeated sunburn might cause skin cancer, premature aging, and wrinkles. Nutrients related to wound healing are also important in the healing of burned skin. These include vitamin C, vitamin A, zinc, folic acid, vitamin B_{12}, other B vitamins, vitamin E, and protein.

Summary

Regardless of the skin condition, or whether the plan is prevention or treatment, the best strategy is a nutritious diet of whole grain breads and cereals, dried beans and peas, lean meats, fresh fruits and vegetables, and low-fat dairy foods. It is the combination of foods in the diet, not one or two nutrients, that provides the best protection against disorders of the skin, hair, and nails.

Nutritional Cosmetics

Food provides nourishment through intestinal absorption and metabolic processes within each cell. Certain foods, in addition to their nutrient content, can be beneficial when applied to the skin. Apples contain a compound called malic acid that is a natural moisturiser. The lactic acid in sour milk, the citric acid in oranges, and the glycolic acid from sugar cane are also natural moisturisers. Ingredients in lemon might bleach and lighten skin colour. Vitamins, minerals, and proteins, however, are too large to be absorbed through the tiny pores of the skin or hair and topical application with food cannot be expected to "nourish" the body.

Is Your Diet Good For Your Skin, Hair And Nails?

Use the following checklist of foods and dietary habits to assess how nourishing your daily diet is for your skin, hair, and nails.

Basics

- Two to three servings of protein foods, such as fish, poultry, lean meat, dried beans, and dried peas.
- One tablespoon of polyunsaturated oil, such as safflower, sunflower, corn, or soy.
- Six or more servings of whole grain breads, cereals, and grains.
- Six to eight glasses of water or other non-diuretic fluids, such as juices, herbal tea, or roasted grain beverages.
- Adequate calorie intake to maintain ideal body weight (1,600 to 2,100 calories for an adult woman; at least 1,200 calories for a woman on a diet; 2,300 to 3,100 calories for a man; at least 1,500 calories for a man on a diet.)

Vitamins

- One to two servings of vitamin A-rich fruits and vegetables, such as carrots, apricots, cantaloupe melon, spinach, or romaine lettuce.
- A vitamin E source, such as one table-

spoon cold pressed oil, wheat germ, or dark green leafy vegetables.

- One to two servings of vitamin C-rich fruits and vegetables, such as oranges, grapefruit, cantaloupe, strawberries, cabbage, potatoes, green pepper, kiwi fruit, tomatoes, broccoli, or dark green leafy vegetables.
- Several servings of vitamin B-rich foods, such as whole grain breads and cereals, dried beans and peas, lean meat, nonfat milk, tuna, nuts, dark green leafy vegetables, or wheat germ.
- One to two servings of folic acid-rich foods, such as dark green leafy vegetables, wheat germ, dried beans and peas, asparagus, or broccoli.
- Weekly exposure to sunlight or a daily serving of vitamin D fortified milk or supplement.

Minerals

- Two or more servings of iron-rich foods, such as lean meat, dark turkey, dried beans and peas, raisins, dried prunes, or potatoes.
- Two to four servings of low-fat or

nonfat milk or milk products, such as low-fat or nonfat milk, low-fat cottage cheese, part skimmed milk cheeses, yoghurt, or other calcium-rich sources, such as dark green leafy vegetables, or calcium supplements.

- Two or more servings of zinc-rich foods, such as lean meat, seafood, poultry, or whole grain breads and cereals.
- Low sodium intake. Limit processed and canned foods, condiments, pickles, canned soups, baking mixes, and salt.

Extras

- Limit intake of alcohol, coffee, black tea, and caffeine-containing soft drinks.
- Limit sugar intake.

Glossary

Acne: An inflammatory disease of the oil-producing glands of the skin.

Amino Acid: A building block of protein; over 20 amino acids are used by the body to form proteins in hair, skin, blood, nails, and other tissues.

Anaemia: A reduction in the number, size, or colour of red blood cells, which results in reduced oxygen carrying capacity of the blood.

Antibody: Compounds in the tissues and fluids that defend the body against foreign substances such as viruses and bacteria.

Anticoagulant: An agent that inhibits blood clotting.

Antioxidant: A compound that protects other compounds or tissues from oxygen fragments by reacting with oxygen.

Calorie: A measurement of heat. In nutrition, calorie refers to the quantity of energy contained in foods.

Capillary: A minute blood vessel that connects the arteries and veins and releases oxygen and nutrients to the tissues while absorbing the waste products from the tissues.

Carotene: The form of vitamin A found in plants.

Cheilosis: Scaling on the lips and cracks at the corners of the mouth caused by a vitamin B_2 deficiency.

Collagen: The supportive substance that holds cells together in connective tissue, skin, tendons, bones, and other tissues.

Connective tissue: A tissue found in every organ that holds together and binds the various tissues in that organ.

Corium: The skin or dermis.

Cortex: The layer of an organ or tissue that lies directly below the outer surface.

Cuticle: A thin layer of skin covering the base of the nail or the outer covering of the hair shaft.

Dermatitis: Inflammation of the skin that can appear as a rash, sore, discolouration, eruption, or ulcer.

Dermis: The skin or corium.

Diuretic: An agent that increases the flow of urine.

Enzyme: A protein produced by the body that initiates and accelerates chemical reactions.

Epidermis: The outer layer of the skin.

Essential nutrient: A substance required for health that cannot be made by the body and must be obtained from the diet.

Follicle: A small cavity or gland in the skin.

Free radical: A highly reactive compound derived from air pollution, radiation, cigarette smoke, or the incomplete breakdown of proteins and fats. Free radicals react with fats in the cell membranes and change their shape or function.

Hormone: A chemical substance produced by a group of cells or an organ, called an endocrine gland, that is released into the blood and transported to another organ or tissue, where it performs a specific action. Examples of hormones include insulin, oestrogen, testosterone, and adrenalin.

Immune system: A complex system of interlocking substances and tissues that protects the body from disease.

Insulin: A hormone that regulates blood sugar and is produced and secreted by the pancreas.

Intrinsic factor: A substance secreted by

the stomach and required for the absorption of vitamin B_{12}.

Keratin: A hard protein substance that forms nails, hair, and some skin tissue.

Lunala: The white half-moon-shaped area at the base of the nail.

Lymph: A transparent fluid contained in the lymphatic vessels. It contains colourless fluids from the blood and is responsible for removing toxins and waste from the tissues and cells.

Mineral: An inorganic substance that is found naturally in the soil.

Obesity: Body weight more than 20% above desirable weight; excess body fat.

Oedema: The presence of abnormally large amounts of fluid in the tissues, especially in the subcutaneous tissues.

Polyunsaturated fat: A type of unsaturated fat that has more than one place where additional hydrogen atoms could be added.

Psoriasis: A chronic inflammation of the skin, especially on the scalp and body, characterised by the development of red patches covered by white scales.

Retinoic acid: A synthetic form of vitamin A.

Saturated fat: A type of fat that contains the maximum number of hydrogen atoms and is said to be "saturated" with hydrogen. Saturated fats are hard at room temperature. Examples are lard, butter, and margarine.

Sebaceous: A tissue that secretes an oily lubricant. Sebaceous glands in the skin secrete oils to moisten hair, skin, and nails.

Sebum: The oily substance secreted by sebaceous glands.

Steatorrhoea: Excess excretion of fat in the stool.

Subcutaneous: Located beneath the skin.

Tryptophan: An amino acid in the diet

that the body uses to produce serotonin and niacin.

Unsaturated Fat: A type of fat that has one or more spots where additional hydrogen atoms could be added. Unsaturated fats are liquid at room temperature and are found primarily in vegetables and vegetable oils.

Vitamin: An essential nutrient required by the body in minute amounts that must be obtained from foods.

Personal Nutrition Notes

Use this space to note the nutritional values of your own favourite foods. Do they make a valuable contribution to your diet?

Personal Diet Notes

Copy this page to keep your own diet diary.

Monday
_____
_____
_____

Tuesday
_____
_____
_____

Wednesday
_____
_____
_____

Thursday
_____
_____
_____

Friday
_____
_____
_____

Saturday
_____
_____
_____

Sunday
_____
_____
_____

Index